Dedication

This journal is dedicated to

YOU!

We hope this journal empowers you to get GRIT so that you can enjoy positive friendships, be happy, dream big and achieve anything you set your mind to.

ISBN 978-0-6482055-9-3 (Paperback Edition)
ISBN 978-0-6482055-1-7 (eBook Edition)

Published by Learning Bug Pty Ltd

First Printing October 2018
Learning Bug Pty Ltd
Brisbane, Australia

GET IN TOUCH
Web: www.getgritprogram.com
Email: info@getgritprogram.com

This Journal Belongs to

....

What Does a Kid with GRIT Look Like?

 Kids with GRIT have a positive attitude and a growth mindset. They believe they can do anything they set their minds to.

 Kids with GRIT never give up. They believe that challenges will make them smarter and they believe that mistakes are proof that they are trying.

 Kids with GRIT are persistent and resilient. They dream big and work hard towards making those dreams come true.

 Kids with GRIT know that they are the boss of their thoughts and their feelings. They manage their anger, frustrations and worries and bounce back from difficulties.

 Kids with GRIT catch negative *I Can't* thoughts that stop them enjoying their day and change them into positive *I Can* thoughts.

 Kids with GRIT maintain friendships by sharing, taking turns, and being honest and trustworthy. Kids with GRIT don't play to win the game but to win friendships.

 Finally, kids with GRIT know how to stand up for themselves and are confident, courageous and brave.

Are you ready to Get GRIT?

How to Use the Get GRIT Journal.

One.

Find a journal mate. A journal mate is a family member or a friend who can share your Get GRIT journey with you. Your journal mate might be your mother, father, grandmother, aunt, uncle or friend.

My journal mate is _____

Two.

Pick a time. Together, choose a time to meet each week to work through your journal together.

We will meet every _____ at _____

Three.

Enjoy your time together! Share stories together, laugh together and have fun!

A Note to Your Journal Mate

Get GRIT is a self-guided journal that teaches kids the knowledge and skills to maintain a healthy mind and positive well-being.

The child's age and ability will determine the level of scaffolding required from their journal mate. Appropriate adjustments may need to be made such as reading the instructions, explaining unknown words or scribing. Dyslexia friendly paragraphs are shaded light blue to reduce visual stress. The journal is not about a child's reading and writing skills but about nurturing strong mental health and well-being by empowering children with the knowledge and skills to be resilient, to enjoy healthy and positive relationships, to tackle life's challenges with grit and to reach their true potential. Get GRIT is about learning essential life skills that support well-being and positive mental health.

Your Role as Journal Mate

You play a very important role as a journal mate. Your role is to share in the child's journaling experience by:

1. Engaging with the child by encouraging them to reflect on key concepts.
2. Guiding the child through the experience.
3. Listening to their thoughts and feelings.
4. Sharing your own experiences.

Mantras

Mantras are positive 'I Can' thoughts that will hopefully become part of your child's internal dialogue. Repeating mantras at home will cement these thoughts in your child and will encourage a growth mindset. My mantras can be found as colouring-in pages and as quotes throughout the journal.

What is GRIT?

The word 'grit' is often used to describe resilience, perseverance and determination. Get GRIT aims to develop grit and much more. GRIT is an acronym for Getting Along, Building Resilience, Identifying Emotions and Taking Responsibility.

The journal consists of 10 lessons that teaches participants how to:

Get Along

- Establish and build positive relationships
- Maintain friendships
- Work collaboratively
- Negotiate and resolve conflict
- Be assertive and stand up to bullies

Build Resilience

- Persevere and overcome frustrations
- Bounce back from adversities
- Recognise the importance of their internal dialogue
- Recognise how thoughts influence feelings and behaviour

Identify Emotions

- Identify and recognise emotions
- Regulate and manage emotional responses
- Manage anxiety and anger
- Understand others' emotional states and needs (empathy)

Take Responsibility

- Develop a growth mindset
- Make positive and responsible decisions
- Develop self-discipline
- Set goals
- Take risks

YOU HAVE
BRAINS in your head.
You have FEET
in your shoes.
You can steer yourself
In any direction you choose.

-Dr. Seuss-

CONTENTS PAGE

Lesson One

You Are Unique

TODAY
you are you!
THAT IS TRUER
than true.

THERE IS
NO ONE ALIVE
who is youer.
THAN YOU!

−Dr. SEUSS−

All About Me

There is no one in the world like you! We all share similarities, but we also have differences. Can you imagine what it would be like if we were all the same? It would be very boring! Differences make us unique. Draw a 'selfie' of yourself on the phone and answer the following questions.

What do you like most about yourself?

_____

_____

_____

What are you good at?

_____

_____

_____

What makes you unique?

_____

_____

_____

Write down 3 compliments that you have received.

_____

_____

_____

Appreciating Diversity

Complete the Venn Diagram with your journal mate. On one face, draw or write all the things that make you different from your journal mate. On the other face, draw or write all the things that make your journal mate different from you. Now think of similarities that you share and write them in the middle where the faces overlap.

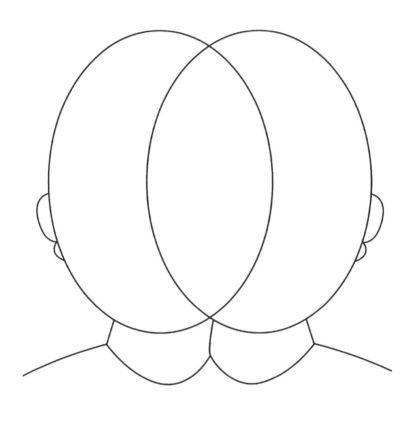

Me _____

Find out who in your family shares similarities with you and who has differences by asking each family member the following questions:

> What is your favourite take-away food?

> What is your favourite week-end activity?

> Where is your favourite place to holiday?

What did you find out?

_____

_____

_____

_____

Why do you think it is important to share similarities?

_____

_____

Why do you think it is important to have differences?

_____

_____

Differences Make Life Interesting and Fun!

Can you think of someone you know who...

Speaks another language? _____

Is really tall? _____

Is good at swimming? _____

Was born in a different country? _____

Wears glasses? _____

Is really old? _____

Rides a bicycle to school? _____

Lives in a different country? _____

Has a pet? _____

Discuss with your journal mate how these differences make life more interesting.

BE YOURSELF.

EVERYONE ELSE
is TAKEN.

Mirror Mirror

We may look different on the outside, but one thing that we all have in common are feelings. It doesn't matter who you are or where you are from, we all experience feelings of happiness and sadness as well as angry feelings and worried feelings. Our body is amazing because it gives us clues to how we are feeling. Draw what happens to your face and body when you feel happy and sad.

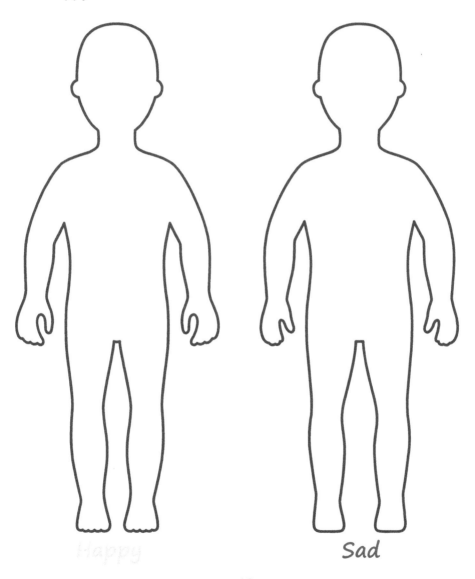

Happy

Sad

All feelings are okay and normal. It is okay to feel angry. It is okay to feel sad and worried too. The most important thing is what you do with your feelings. Draw what happens to your face and body when you are feeling angry and worried.

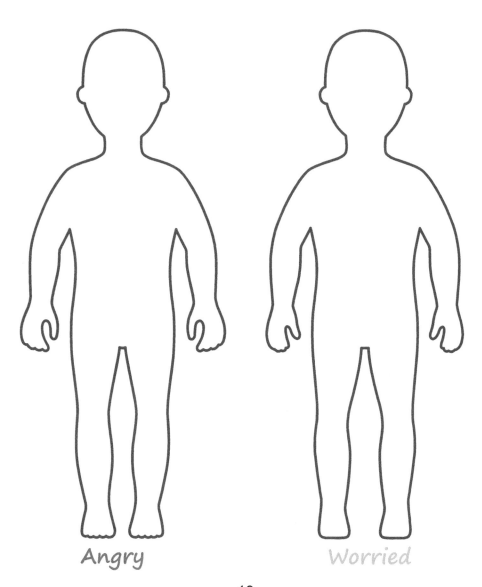

Angry

Worried

Empathy in a Shoebox

A person's face and body can reveal a lot about how they are feeling. If you notice someone looking unhappy, you can acknowledge how they are feeling by saying, 'You look ...', and then you can ask how you could help them. When you are feeling unhappy, it's nice to have someone show that they care about you.

Think of a time you helped someone. What happened?

_____

_____

_____

How do you think they were feeling?

_____

_____

What did you do or say to help them?

_____

_____

_____

How did you feel after helping them?

_____

_____

By putting yourself in 'someone else's shoes' you are able to think about how they are feeling. This is called empathy. Empathy is about understanding other people's feelings.

Now think of a time when someone helped you. What happened?

_____

_____

_____

_____

What did they say or do?

_____

_____

_____

How did you feel after they helped you?

_____

_____

_____

_____

Lesson Two

Take Control

Be who you are and
say what you feel
because those who
mind don't matter
and those who
matter don't mind.

– Dr. Seuss–

Anger

Everyone experiences feelings of anger. Some people experience angry feelings more often than others.

Think of a time when you felt really angry about something. What happened?

_____

_____

_____

Why did you feel so angry?

_____

_____

_____

What was your body doing to tell you that you were angry?

_____

_____

_____

_____

_____

Good Things About Anger

When you become angry, chemicals are released in your brain. These chemicals cause the changes that you feel in your body. These changes make you more alert and give you extra strength and can be useful if you need to protect yourself or if you need to keep yourself safe.

Positive changes have happened in the world because people were angry about an injustice and worked together to change things for the better.

Ask your journal mate if they can think of a positive change that has happened in the world because of someone who got angry. What happened?

_____

_____

_____

_____

Ask your journal mate if they can think of how they have used anger to make life better for themselves or for others.

_____

_____

_____

_____

If used properly, anger can do positive things.

Bad Things About Anger

If anger is not managed properly all sorts of problems can happen.

What could happen if anger is allowed to rage out of control?

_____

_____

_____

_____

Can you think of a time when your angry feelings raged out of control? What happened?

_____

_____

_____

_____

How did you feel after you calmed down?

_____

_____

Always use your words to tell your feelings. It is never okay to hurt someone with your hands, feet or unkind words. High five choices can help you control your angry feelings so that you can keep yourself and others safe.

High Five Choices

Remember all feelings are okay, it's what you do with your feelings that counts. When you are angry or upset, you can make a high five choice. High five choices will help you to take control of your angry feelings. When someone gives you a high five it's because you have done something great! Poor choices, like hitting someone when you are angry, can hurt other people and will make you feel bad too.

How do you calm your angry feelings? On each finger, write 5 high five choices that you can make to take control of your anger.

How do you calm angry feelings and take control of your body? Draw a picture below.

Feelings Thermometer – The Warning Signs

Your body gives you warning signs to signal how you are feeling. While we all experience angry feelings, the warning signs your body gives you may be different to someone else's warning signs. Let's look closely at the warning signs you get at each level on the Feelings Thermometer.

Feelings Thermometer

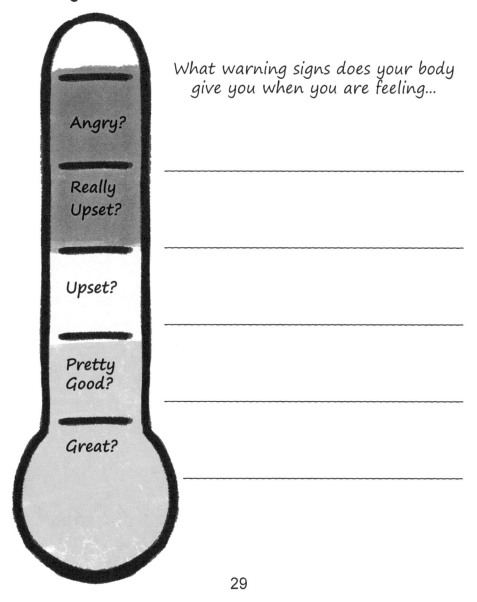

What warning signs does your body give you when you are feeling...

Angry?

Really Upset?

_____

Upset?

_____

Pretty Good?

_____

Great?

_____

Feelings Thermometer

It is much harder to calm angry feelings at the highest
temperature on your Feelings Thermometer. It is much easier to
take control of your feelings when your Feelings Thermometer
is at 'Upset' or 'Really Upset'. If you can recognise the warning
signs, you can take control of your anger before it rages out of
control.

When you feel yourself getting upset, where on your body do
you get your warning signs?

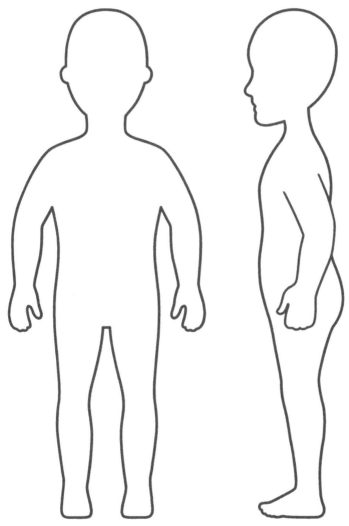

When you are getting really upset where on your body do you get your warning signs? You may feel shaky or sick in the tummy. Your heart may speed up or your muscles may feel tight. Your jaw or your hands may feel tight too. You may also feel like crying. Remember, if you can recognise the warning signs your body gives you when you get really upset, you can control your anger before your Feelings Thermometer reaches **angry.**

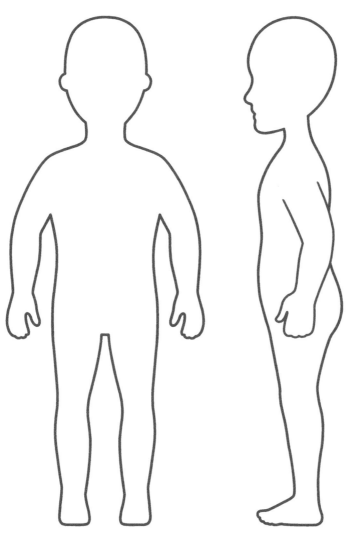

How to Calm Anger

With your journal mate, read through the following high five choices and colour in the high five strategies you would like to try next time you are angry.

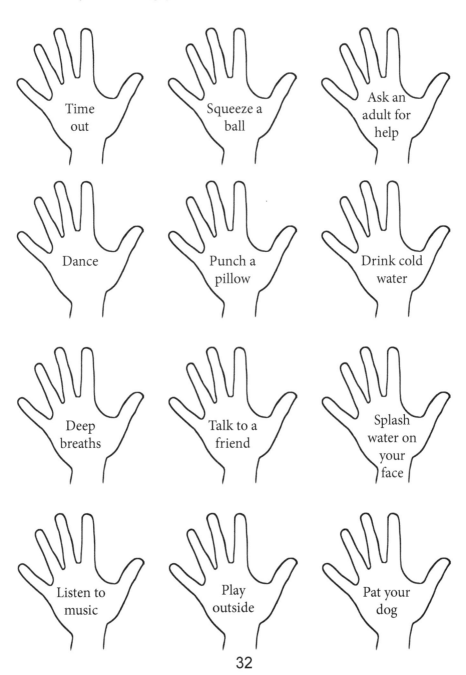

Lowering the Temperature

When you are feeling angry, remember that you have the power over your body to relax and gain control. Listen to your body and when you recognise the warning signs, make a high five choice!

Feelings Thermometer

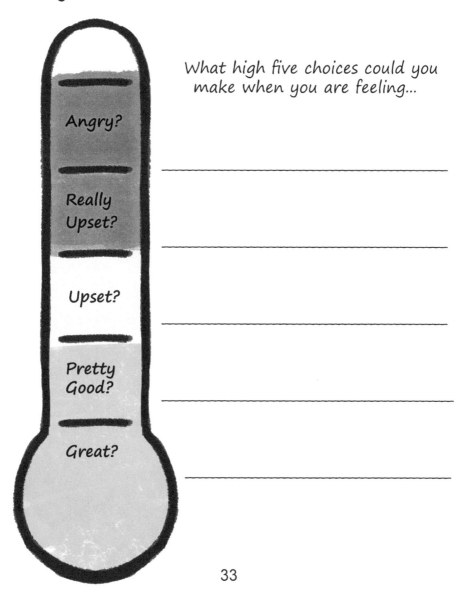

What high five choices could you make when you are feeling...

Angry?

_____

Really Upset?

_____

Upset?

_____

Pretty Good?

_____

Great?

_____

Visualisation

Imagining a special place where you feel happy and relaxed can help you when you are feeling upset. Your special place might be at the beach, at a park or in your favourite room sitting on your favourite chair. Let's practise visualising your favourite place.

Step 1. Close your eyes. Take a deep breath in and out.
Step 2. Imagine yourself in your special place. A place where you feel relaxed and happy. What can you see? What can you hear? What can you smell? How does this special place make you feel? Really focus on that feeling.
Step 3: Open your eyes. How do you feel?

Draw your favourite place below.

Star Breathing

Breathing exercises can calm angry feelings. Intense angry feelings can cloud your judgement, which can sometimes lead to bad decisions. Breathing exercises can help you feel calm so that you can think more clearly and make better choices.

With your finger, follow your way around the star. When you breathe in, take a deep belly breath in through your nose and breathe out through your mouth.

Star Breathing with Your Hand

You can use this calming strategy anywhere. Let's practise star breathing with your hand. Stretch out your hand like a star. Using your pointer finger on your other hand, trace your fingers up and down. When you breathe in, take a deep belly breath in through your nose and slide up each finger. Breathe out through your mouth as you slide down each finger.

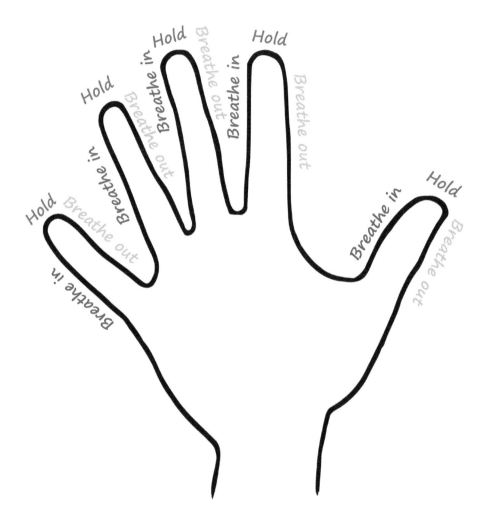

How do you feel now?

Story Massage

Massage relaxes your body and can help you to feel calm again. Massage can be helpful if you are angry or if you are worried. You can always ask a family member to give you a massage or if you see someone in your family feeling upset, you can offer to give them a massage.

Now it's time for you and your journal mate to give each other a story massage. A story massage is a story you tell while giving a massage. You can make up your own story massage.

The Jungle Dance

The beats of the drum call all the animals to the jungle dance.	Gently pound up and down your partner's back.
The monkeys swing in from branch to branch.	Wave hands across back.
The elephants stampede in.	Hands chop across back.
The snakes slither across the ground.	Hands slither up and down back.
The warthogs squeeze through the crowd.	Squeeze shoulders.
Finally the lions walk in proudly.	Hands walk up and down back.
The beats of the jungle drum can be heard from afar as the animals dance to the beats.	Gently pound up and down back.

Pass on Your Smile

A smile is contagious, when someone smiles at you it is hard not to smile back. It's time to play a game with your journal mate. Taking turns, smile your widest, silliest smile at each other to try and make each other giggle or laugh. You get a point if the other person can't keep a totally straight face. Record a point every time you or your journal mate make each other smile.

Smiling Tally

Me	My Journal Mate

A challenge for you and your journal mate!

Always remember how powerful a smile can be and how it can make someone feel. See how many people you can pass your smile on to this week!

If you see SOMEONE
without a SMILE,
give them one of yours.

– Dolly Parton–

Lesson Three

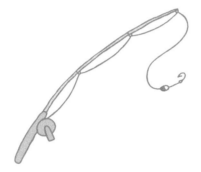

Catch Your Thoughts

If you have
GOOD THOUGHTS
they will shine out of your face
like SUNBEAMS and
you will always look lovely.

-Roald Dahl-

Guess My Thoughts

No one can hear the talking in your head. Only you! We have thoughts all the time and we usually don't pay a lot of attention to them. Our thoughts are powerful and influence how we feel and what we do. You are going to learn how to slow down your thoughts and pay attention to the talking in your head.

Ask your journal mate to think of something. Now see if you can guess what they are thinking about.

What did you guess? _____

What was your journal mate thinking about?

_____

It is hard isn't it! That's because you are the only person who can hear the talking in your head.

Do you know what I'm thinking? I'm thinking that you don't know what I'm thinking.

Thoughts versus Feelings

Our thoughts are different to our feelings. Write or draw some
of your thoughts in the thought bubble and write and draw some
of your feelings in the heart.

I'm not going.

I have no friends.

Frustrated.

What a
lovely day!

Happy.

Worried.

What if I forget
my homework
book?

That is not fair.

Pause for a moment and put your journal aside. Sit quietly with your journal mate. After a couple of minutes share with each other what you were thinking about and how your thoughts were making you feel. Draw or write below what you were thinking about.

_____

_____

_____

How did you feel?

_____

_____

_____

How do you think you would feel if you were thinking the following thoughts? Write your answer in the heart.

I Can and I Can't Thoughts

If you pay attention to the talking in your head, it is possible to listen to what you are saying to yourself. You can catch these messages to see if they are *I Can* thoughts or *I Can't* thoughts. Our thoughts are very powerful. Changing the way we think can change the way we feel.

I Can't thoughts are negative messages that stop us from having fun and doing our best.

Can you think of some *I Can't* thoughts? Write them below.

_____

_____

_____

_____

I Can thoughts are positive messages that help us to be the best we can be and enjoy our day.

Can you think of some *I Can* thoughts? Write them below.

_____

_____

_____

_____

_____

Changing the way you think and learning how to talk to yourself in a helpful way can change the way you feel. So think happy!

Colour the *I Can* thoughts in yellow **and the** *I Can't* thoughts in red.

Draw *I Can* thoughts in the box below.

I Can Thoughts

Think of some positive *I Can* statements to write in the shield. Practise saying the *I Can* statements to protect you against negative I *Can't* thoughts.

Look out for mantras throughout your journal. Mantras are positive thoughts that you can say to yourself to change your mindset.

Think of a time recently when you were feeling **angry.** What happened?

_____

_____

What were you thinking? Was it an _I Can't_ thought or an _I Can_ thought?

_____

_____

What did you do?

_____

Think of a time recently when you were feeling **worried.** What happened?

_____

_____

What were you thinking? Was it an _I Can't_ thought or an _I Can_ thought?

_____

_____

What did you do?

_____

Throughout the week, try to catch your thoughts and record any negative *I Can't* thoughts you have below. Record the positive *I Can* thoughts you have on the next page.

I Can't Thoughts

I Can Thoughts

Lesson Four

Change Your Mindset

Believe you CAN and
you're half-way there.

Theodore Roosevelt

Whether You Think You Can or Can't, You're Right!

The school cross country race was fast approaching. Sammy and his class practised running around the oval every day. Sammy believed he was no good at running. The day of the big race finally arrived, Sammy and his friends lined up ready to start the race. The whistle sounded and the children were off and running. Sammy started running as fast as he could. But he soon became tired and started walking. Sammy didn't finish the race.

What happened to Sammy during his race?

_____

_____

_____

_____

What do you think Sammy was thinking during his race?

_____

_____

Were Sammy's thoughts *I Can* thoughts or *I Can't* thoughts?

_____

_____

How do you think he was feeling?

_____

_____

How did Sammy's thoughts influence what he did?

_____

_____

How We Think Influences How We Act

The talking in our head not only influences how we feel, but also how we act. With your journal mate, read through the following scenarios. Write how you would feel in the heart and how you would act in the circle if you were thinking the following thoughts.

It starts raining just before lunch time and you think to yourself, 'I hate playing inside'.

You are trying to finish your homework and you think to yourself, 'This is too hard'.

Your friend is away and you have no one to play with. You think to yourself, 'I have no one to play with'.

You are finishing off a really challenging maths problem and you think to yourself, 'If I keep trying, I will work it out'.

What is a Mindset?

Our mindset is made up of our beliefs about how smart we are. We have just learned about how powerful our thoughts are and how they can influence how we feel and how we behave. Our beliefs about how smart we are influence what we can achieve.

Our mindset is made up of what we think we can do and what we think we can't do!

A growth mindset is when you believe, that through practice, persistence and effort, you can achieve anything you set your mind to.

In the 'growth mindset' head, think of positive *I Can* thoughts that will lead to a growth mindset. In the 'fixed mindset' head, think of negative *I Can't* thoughts that will lead to a fixed mindset.

A fixed mindset is when you believe that how smart you are is fixed and cannot change.

Train Your Brain - Watch it Grow

Your brain is like a muscle in your body. When you exercise, your muscles become stronger. When you learn new things, your brain becomes stronger too. Your brain grows and gets stronger every time you learn something new, especially if it's challenging! That's when you really stretch your brain. Just like trees need water to grow, your brain needs to learn and be challenged in order to grow and become stronger.

Think of something that you are really good at and write it below.

_____

_____

What did you do in order to be good at it? How did you train your brain to be good at it?

_____

_____

Now think of something that you would like to become better at.

_____

_____

What can you do to train your brain to make you better at it?

_____

_____

_____

_____

Grow Your Mind

The first thing you need to know is that your intelligence isn't fixed and that it can change. It can get stronger or weaker depending on how much effort you are willing to make.

I can't do it.   I want to do it.   How do I do it?   I will try to do it.   I can do it.

How can you grow your mind?

_____

_____

_____

_____

Stretching Your Brain

Your brain stretches and grows when you exercise it. How do you exercise your brain? By taking on a challenge!

Think of something that you did recently that was challenging for you. What was it?

_____

_____

What were you thinking while you were working on the challenge?

_____

_____

How did you feel?

_____

Did you make any mistakes while you were working on the challenge? What mistakes did you make?

_____

_____

What did you learn from your mistake?

_____

_____

MY BRAIN is LIKE A MUSCLE

IT GROWS AND GETS STRONGER THE MORE I USE IT

A Glass Half Full

The school bell rang as the children finished packing their bags. Ethan and Ava walked home after a busy day at school. Arriving home, Ethan's dad asked him how his day went. 'It was a terrible day', Ethan told his dad, 'My best friend was sick today. It rained all day so we couldn't play outside and the science experiment was cancelled'. When Ava arrived home, her dad asked how her day went. Ava told her dad, 'It rained outside so we got to play games inside. The science experiment was cancelled so our teacher organised an art activity, and my friend was away so I played with some new friends. It was a great day'.

A 'glass half full' is an expression that describes someone who is positive and optimistic. If they had a glass of water that was half-filled, they would look at their glass and say that it is half full. A person who is negative will look at the glass and say that it was half empty.

In the story, who had a 'glass half full' attitude? Why?

_____

_____

_____

In the story, who had a 'glass half empty' attitude? Why?

_____

_____

_____

Can you remember a time when you had a glass half full attitude? What happened?

_____

_____

_____

Ask your journal mate if they can think of a time when they had a glass half full attitude.

The 'If, Then' Attitude TRAP!

Don't fall into the 'If, Then' attitude trap! This trap can stop you from enjoying your day and being grateful.

What is the 'If, Then' attitude trap?

Have you ever thought?

If I get an iPad, **then** I'll be happy.
If I get into the basketball team, **then** I'll be happy.
If I get a brand new game, **then** I'll be happy.

Have you ever had an 'If, Then' attitude? What was it?

_____

_____

_____

_____

Ask your journal mate to think of a time when they had an 'If, Then' attitude.

Have a Gratitude Attitude!

A gratitude attitude focuses on the NOW! Try to pay attention and be thankful for what you already have and not worry about what you don't have. People with a gratitude attitude are positive, resilient and happy.

A Gratitude Attitude

Every day this week, write down something that you are thankful for and place it in an empty jar. At the end of the week, read all the things that you are grateful for. You may like to share your gratitude jar with your family.

Feeling gratitude and not expressing it is like wrapping a present and not giving it.

– William Arthur Ward–

Mindful Minutes

Mindfulness is about being aware of your thoughts and your feelings. It is also about being aware of your surroundings and being present in the moment. Most importantly, it is about being calm. Try practising mindful minutes throughout your day to help your mind and body stay calm and happy.

I am paying attention to my breathing.
In through my nose and out through my mouth.
I will let any thoughts come and go. If my mind wanders,
I can just come back to my breathing.

I am paying attention to my surroundings.
What can I hear? What can I smell? What can I see?
How am I feeling?
I am in control of my thoughts and feelings.

Today was a Great Day!

Think about your day today and answer the following questions.

Today I am thankful for: _____

_____

The best part of my day was: _____

_____

I felt happy today when: _____

_____

I can make tomorrow great by: _____

_____

Next time someone asks how your day was, start with the
positive things that happened during the day.

Try to answer these questions every day!

71

Lesson Five

Yet

The Power of Yet

It's not impossible it's I'm possible!

Think of all the things that you can already do and write or draw them in the circles below. Now think of something that you can't do yet. Yet is a really important word! You can set goals to learn how to do something that you can't do yet and with a growth mindset, anything is possible.

Things I can already do...

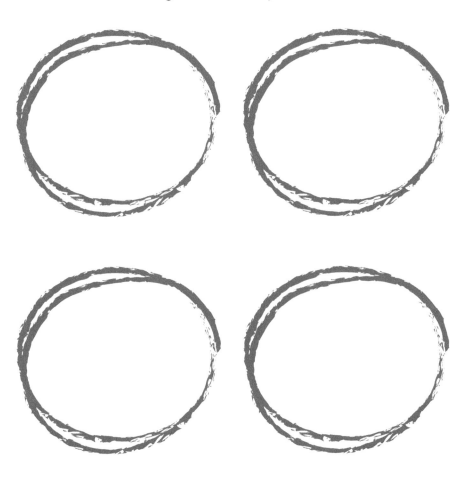

I Can't

YET!

But I will keep trying until I can!

I Can Achieve Anything

When you want to learn something new, it helps to break up your goal into small achievable steps. Think of something you would like to learn.

I would like to learn to _____

What do you need to do to achieve your goal? Break your goal down into steps. Draw or write each step in the boxes below.

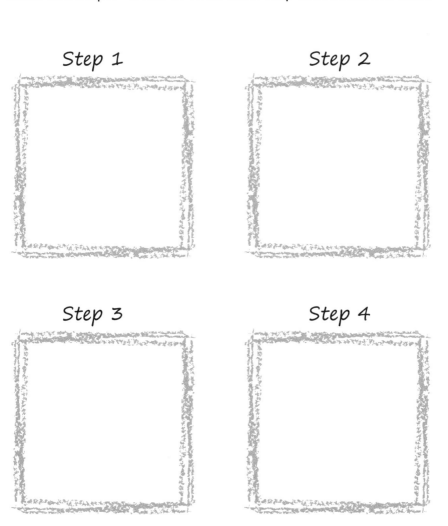

Step 1

Step 2

Step 3

Step 4

MISTAKES ARE PROOF THAT YOU ARE TRYING

Risk Taking

Good learners go into the Learning Pit. What is the Learning Pit? It is where you go to challenge your brain. It is where true learning happens. Sometimes you may be scared to go into the Learning Pit because you are worried that you may make a mistake.

Think of a time you recently made a mistake. What happened?

_____

_____

What did you learn from your mistake?

_____

_____

Think of a time you recently challenged your brain and went into the Learning Pit. What happened?

_____

_____

What did you learn?

_____

_____

How did you feel?

_____

_____

The Learning Pit

Ask your journal mate to share a time they recently took on a challenge.

A Positive Attitude.

Someone with a positive attitude has *I Can* thoughts. They see the glass as half full. Having a positive attitude is very important as it helps you when you are facing difficulties or hardships. A positive attitude is also very important when you are learning.

With your journal mate, complete the following calculations to see how important your attitude is when it comes to learning.

If

A=1, B=2, C=3, D=4, E=5, F=6, G=7, H=8, I=9, J=10, K=11, L=12, M=13, N=14, O=15, P=16, Q=17, R=18, S=19, T=20, U=21, V=22, W=23, X=24, Y=25, Z=26

THEN

Knowledge = 11+14+15+23+12+5+4+7+5 = 96%

AND

Hard work = _____ =   %

Knowledge and hard work are very important for learning. They both fall short of 100%. Can you and your journal mate calculate what attitude adds up to?

ATTITUDE = _____ =   %

Effort Meter

Use the effort meter to help you think about how much effort you put in to an activity. Think of an activity you did today at school or at home and answer the following questions.

Using the effort meter, how much effort did you put in?

_____

If you need to put more effort in, what can you do to improve?

_____

_____

_____

_____

_____

Effort Meter

Dream Big!

What do you dream of doing or becoming when you are older?
Draw a picture of your dream below.

You can achieve anything you set your mind to. What do you need to learn to accomplish your dream?

_____

_____

_____

_____

_____

_____

_____

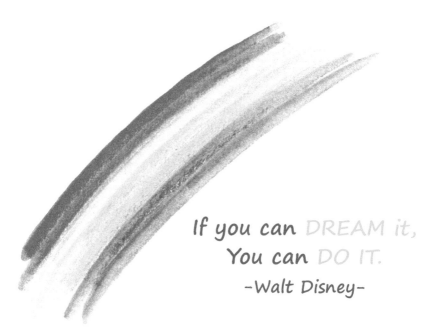

If you can DREAM it,
You can DO IT.
-Walt Disney-

7 Day Positivity Challenge

Can you complete the 7 day positivity challenge? These 7 challenges are a sure way to make you feel great!

Write down 5 things you like about yourself. ☐

Describe and draw the best part of your day. ☐

Try something new that you have never done before. ☐

Do something kind and helpful for someone. ☐

Draw something that you are grateful for. ☐

Draw a picture for someone special. ☐

Ask your teacher for work that will challenge your brain! ☐

What Did I Learn this Week?

What did you learn at school this week?

_____

_____

_____

_____

Draw or write down the bits you don't get YET.

What mistakes did you make that helped you learn?

_____

_____

_____

_____

What can you do to improve?

_____

_____

_____

_____

How will you be a good learner this week?

_____

_____

_____

_____

_____

PRACTICE MAKES PROGRESS

Lesson Six

Worry Bullies

Worry gives a small
thing a BIG shadow.

Swedish Proverb

Why Worry?

Worry and fear are very important emotions. These emotions prepare you for **real** danger. The part of your brain responsible for checking if you are safe is called the amygdala (ah-mig-dah-la). The amygdala acts like an alarm in your brain. When you are worried or scared your amygdala turns on the alarm and your body will respond by running away, fighting back or freezing. When the amygdala alarm is turned on it can be hard to think clearly.

Imagine you are walking through a forest and you see a bear walking towards you.

What would you do?

_____

What would your journal mate do?

_____

You may have a different answer to your journal mate. Would you run away from the bear? Or would you try and scare the bear away? Or would you freeze?

Your body responds to danger by either fleeing (running away from the bear), fighting (trying to scare the bear) or freezing (hoping that the bear won't see you if you stand really still). When you worry your body also responds in one of these ways.

Do you remember a time when you were worried or scared about something? How did you respond?

_____

_____

_____

When Worry Becomes a Problem

Worry becomes a problem when your body is preparing for **real** danger, but the danger is not real and/or is unlikely. Sometimes your brain prepares you for danger, and sends you the signals to run away, fight back or freeze, but the danger is not real. A bear walking toward you is a real danger, but a monster under your bed is not a real danger, and a natural disaster is an unlikely danger.

What would be a real danger?

_____

_____

_____

What would be an unreal or unlikely danger?

_____

_____

_____

False Alarm!

A fire alarm warns us of danger. If there was a fire, the fire alarm would sound to alert us, so we could run away. A smoke alarm that is too sensitive may go off when there is no real danger. Sometimes we worry more than we need to. We are like a sensitive fire alarm. If we had a sensitive fire alarm we would fix it. If you are worrying a lot, you have the power to fix it so that your worries are not stopping you from enjoying your day.

My Worry Cloud

Sometimes, your worries may feel like a dark cloud hanging over you. Draw or write any worries that you have in the first cloud. Ask your journal mate to write down any worries they have in the second cloud.

The Warning Signs

When you are feeling worried or anxious where on your body do you get your warning signs? You may feel sick or feel like you have butterflies in your tummy. You may feel shaky, or your skin may become clammy. Your heart may start beating faster.

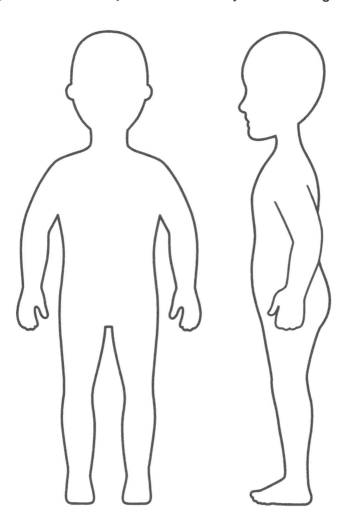

Slow, deep breathing will help calm worried feelings so that you can take control of your body. Thinking positive 'I Can' thoughts will also help you fight any worry bullies.

What is a Worry Bully?

Fighting worries is hard work. You have the power to make your worries go away. Worries are like bullies. Unless you stand up to them they won't go away. A worry bully is a negative *I Can't* thought that stops you from having fun and enjoying your day. Worry bullies are mean and ugly. Imagine what a worry bully looks like and draw it below.

My  bully

Be on the Look Out for Worry Bullies!

Don't let worry bullies ruin your day! Here are some common worry bullies that you can be on the look out for.

 Bother you all night and day.

 Use words like 'always' or 'never'.

 Lie to make you scared.

 Lie and tell you things that have not even happened and most likely won't happen.

 Imagine things that aren't real.

 Exaggerate how bad something will be.

 Stop you from giving things a go!

Worry Bully VERSUS Truth

Worry bullies lie to make you scared or to make you worry about something that has not even happened and, most likely, will never happen. These thoughts can lead you to believe that things are worse than they actually are. Worry bullies focus on the worst possible outcome. In the thought clouds think of worrying thoughts you have had or are having and then try to challenge these thoughts by thinking about what is actually true.

How Big is My Problem?

Worry bullies can exaggerate how bad something will be. Use the 'How Big is My Problem' scale to help you keep things in perspective. Sometimes you might make a problem bigger than it is. You need to ask yourself, is it terrible or is it just a tad bad? Draw pictures of what you think would be terrible, very bad, bad, a little bad or a tad bad next to the scale.

Terrible

Very bad

Bad

A little bad

A tad bad

Worry Bullies STOP You!

Worry Bullies can stop you from having a go by using words like 'always' and 'never' to describe situations. For example, 'I always make mistakes' or 'I never get a turn'. This often stops you from risk taking, persevering and enjoying your day with your friends.

Can you remember a time when your thoughts stopped you from **giving something a go?** What happened?

_____

_____

_____

_____

_____

Can you remember a time when your thoughts stopped you from **enjoying your day?** What happened?

_____

_____

_____

_____

_____

Ask your journal mate to share a time when their thoughts stopped them from giving something a go.

Jumping to Conclusions

You jump to conclusions when you predict what is going to happen, with little or with no evidence. For example you might think, 'My teacher is going to send me to the office tomorrow because I forgot my library books'. Jumping to conclusions can also involve thinking that you know what others are thinking; we call this mind-reading. Mind-reading happens when you believe that you know what others are thinking. Often we assume that they are thinking the worst of us.

Can you think of a time when you jumped to a conclusion? What happened?

_____

_____

_____

_____

Did what you predict would happen, actually happen?

_____

_____

_____

Can you think of a time when you thought you knew what someone else was thinking? What happened?

_____

_____

_____

Stand Up to Your Worries!

 1. Draw a picture of your worry or put your worry into words by telling an adult or friend.

 2. Question the worry. Ask yourself, 'Is it really that bad?' Remind yourself that bad things don't happen very often. Even if it is terrible, you can handle it.

 3. Stand up to your worry. Don't let the worry bully you. You need to stand up to your worry in order for it to go away. You could say to your worry...

It's not that bad.

I don't believe you!

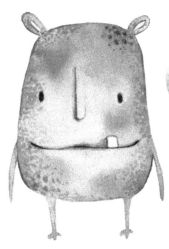

Leave me alone.

You don't know if that's true.

What else could you say to your worry bully?

My Worries

Choose a worry you have at the moment or you have recently had.

What were you worried about?

_____

_____

How did you feel?

_____

_____

What was your body doing to tell you that you were worried?

_____

_____

On the *How Big is My Problem?* scale, how big did you think your worry was at the time?

_____

Now looking back, was your worry as big as you thought it was? What happened?

_____

_____

Lesson Seven

Mission Friendship

The ONLY way to have a friend
IS TO BE ONE.

– Ralph Waldo Emerson-

Getting Along

When we get along with our friends we enjoy our day and have fun. Learning to get along with friends is one of the important reasons why you go to school. We go to school to learn to read and write and we also go to school to learn how to get along with other people.

What does it mean to get along?

_____

_____

_____

_____

_____

It is important to remember that we need to get along with people we may not necessary like.

Why do you think it is important to get along with everyone?

_____

_____

_____

_____

To Have a Friend is to Be a Friend

What makes a good friend? Think of a friend you have now or you used to have and write their name below.

My friend: _____

What are 3 things that *make or made* this person a great friend?

_____

_____

_____

Draw a picture of you and your friend.

Recipe for a Great Friend

What makes a good friend? Remember the only way to have a great friend is to be a great friend. This means that you need to practise friendly behaviours with your friends. If we show others that we are friendly, they will want to play with us.

What makes a great friend?

Recipe for a Great Friend

A cup of _____

A drop of _____

A teaspoon of _____

A sprinkle of _____

Mix together with _____

Bake for 30 minutes _____

Serve with _____

What Makes a Good Friend?

Colour in the puzzle pieces that describe the type of friend you would like to have and the type of friend you would like to be.

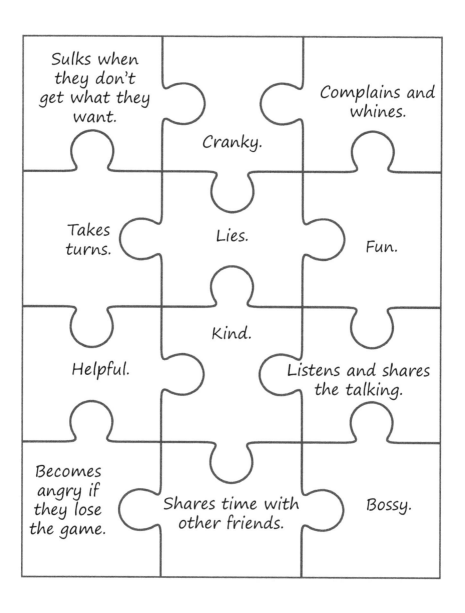

People come into
our lives
for a reason,
a season,
or a lifetime.

A Reason, A Season, A Lifetime

Have you ever been friends with someone that you are no longer friends with anymore? What happened?

_____

_____

_____

_____

What did you enjoy about your friendship?

_____

_____

_____

_____

Why do you think you are not friends anymore?

_____

_____

_____

Ask your journal mate to tell you about a friend who they are no longer friends with.

Friendly or Unfriendly Behaviour

How would you feel if this happened to you?

You tell your friend something private and ask them not to tell anyone. You find out that your friend told someone else.

How would you feel? _____

Is this friendly or unfriendly behaviour? _____

. . . .

You and your friend are playing snakes and ladders; your friend rolls the dice and quickly changes it to a higher number.

How would you feel? _____

Is this friendly or unfriendly behaviour? _____

. . . .

You are spending your lunch break in the library, your friend sees another friend and leaves the library without telling you.

How would you feel? _____

Is this friendly or unfriendly behaviour? _____

Some older kids start calling you names. Your friend comes over and tells them to stop calling you names.

How would you feel? _____

Is this friendly or unfriendly behaviour? _____

. . . .

You are playing a game of handball with your friend. Your friend wins and 'rubs it in' by clapping and yelling, 'I win, you lose'.

How would you feel? _____

Is this friendly or unfriendly behaviour? _____

. . . .

You are playing a game of soccer at playtime. Your friend loses the game, so they sulk and stop talking to you.

How would you feel? _____

Is this friendly or unfriendly behaviour? _____

. . . .

You get a lot of your spelling words wrong in your spelling test. Your friend asks you if they can help you learn your words.

How would you feel? _____

Is this friendly or unfriendly behaviour? _____

When a Friend Treats You Badly

Have you ever been friends with someone who wasn't treating you like a true friend? What happened?

_____

_____

_____

_____

_____

Is it okay to stop being friends with someone? Why?

_____

_____

_____

_____

*Ask your journal mate to
share a time when a friend
treated them badly.*

Mission Friendship

It is important to be a good friend. You are unique and you have special talents and interests. It is important to remember that you can have different friends who may share your different interests. You may have friends at school, in your neighbourhood, at your tennis club, drama club or in your family. You may like to have a best friend, but it is good to have other friends too. You can still be friends with someone and play with other people too.

How can you be a good friend?

_____

_____

_____

_____

_____

_____

_____

_____

_____

How to Make a New Friend

If you have no one to play with, you need to be brave and make a new friend. The way you choose to join in on a game can look friendly or unfriendly. If you act in a friendly way, others will more likely want you to join in.

What could you say to your new friend or friends?

How could you show that you are friendly?

_____

_____

_____

_____

If you are joining a game, why is it important to listen carefully to follow the rules of the game?

_____

_____

_____

_____

Mission Friendship - Making a New Friend!

My mission is to make a new friend with _____

If you have someone in mind, write their name above.

What will you say?   What will you do?

Mission accomplished!

Did you make a new friend? _____

What game did you play with your new friend?

_____

What do you have in common with your new friend?

_____

_____

Lesson Eight

Working Together

Alone we can do so little
TOGETHER we can do so much.
-Helen Keller-

Parts of a Friend

Ears
Listen and share the talking. Listen to what your friend is saying and show that you are interested by asking questions.

Head
Try to understand your friend by thinking about things from their point of view.

Eyes
Show your friend you are interested in them by looking at them when they are talking.

Mouth
Be honest when you talk to your friend so your friend knows that they can trust you.

Heart
Be aware of your friend's feelings. Try to understand how your friend is feeling.

Hands
Be helpful. Do things to help your friend out.

Winning and Losing Gracefully

The best way to think of winning and losing is to play to win friendship. If you play to win friendship you are more likely to win and lose gracefully. Gracefully means that you are friendly whether you win or lose. If you become angry or sulk when you lose or if you 'rub it in' when you win, your friends won't want to play with you. It is important to win and lose gracefully, which means remembering that winning is not the most important thing. We sometimes win and we sometimes lose, but the most important thing is that we enjoy playing with our friends.

Do you remember a time when you or a friend lost a game and either sulked or became angry? What happened?

_____

_____

_____

Do you remember a time when you or a friend won a game and 'rubbed it in'? What happened?

_____

_____

_____

How did it make you feel?

_____

_____

Winning and Losing Y Chart

What does winning and losing gracefully look like, sound like and feel like? Draw or write what you think winning and losing gracefully looks like, feels like and sounds like on the Y Chart below.

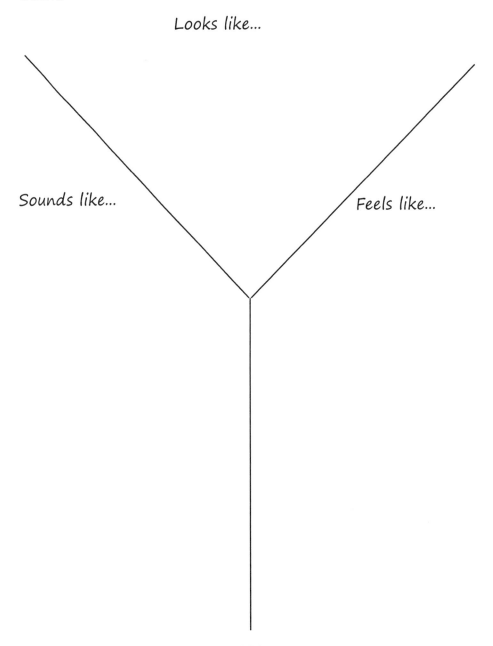

Looks like...

Sounds like...

Feels like...

Play to Win Friendships

Honesty

Honesty is always telling the truth in what you say and what you do. It is important to always be honest. Being honest is one of the most important qualities in a friendship. It's important to be honest with your mother and father, your teacher, and your brothers and sisters. If you are honest, your friends will trust you.

Can you think of a time when you or your friend were not honest? What happened?

_____

_____

_____

_____

_____

How did it make you feel?

_____

_____

_____

_____

_____

Why is it important to be honest with your friends?

_____

_____

_____

_____

Why is it important to be honest with your parents?

_____

_____

_____

_____

Friendship is like a
beautiful garden,

The more you put
into it the more it
grows!

Sharing the Conversation

It is important to listen to your friends and share the talking. To show you are interested in your friend, ask questions. You can also start a conversation by asking a question. You might like to ask a new friend what their favourite game is or what they like to play. Listen carefully when your friends are talking to you. By listening, you can ask more questions and keep the conversation going.

Imagine you have just met a new friend. What could you say?

_____

_____

_____

_____

How could you show you are interested in what your friend is saying?

_____

_____

_____

_____

_____

_____

Lesson Nine

How to Fix a Wrinkled Heart

If we talk about this.
I'm sure we can work it out.

How to Solve a Disagreement

Disagreements are bound to happen in every friendship;
no matter how old you are. Disagreements tend to happen
more when you are a kid, because you and your friends are
still learning the skills to fix problems when you are playing
together.

Do you remember the last time you and a friend had a
disagreement? What happened?

_____

_____

_____

_____

How did you feel?

_____

How do you think your friend felt?

_____

Did you solve the disagreement?

_____

_____

Crocodile, Dog, Rabbit, Turtle and Owl all tackle
disagreements a little differently to each other. You are going to
learn about how each animal takes on a disagreement.

Crocodile

Never smile at a Crocodile because Croc is likely to SNAP! Croc isn't the friendliest of animals. Croc tackles a disagreement by yelling and arguing. Croc can be VERY stubborn and very unhelpful when it comes to a disagreement.

Have you or a friend ever tackled a disagreement like Croc? What happened?

_____

_____

_____

_____

Did you resolve the argument?

_____

_____

_____

How did you feel? _____

How did your friend feel? _____

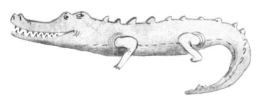

Owl

Owl is wise and tries to sort out the problem. When faced with an argument, Owl works together to find a solution where both sides win.

Have you or a friend ever solved a disagreement like Owl? What happened?

_____

_____

_____

_____

Did you resolve the argument?

_____

_____

_____

How did you feel? _____

How did your friend feel? _____

Turtle

Turtle doesn't like disagreements and hides when there is an argument. Sometimes, walking away for a short period is a good option because if you are angry it can give you time to cool down. However hiding from a disagreement is an unhelpful way to solve a problem because only one person gets what they want and is happy. It doesn't solve the problem.

Have you or a friend ever tackled a disagreement like Turtle? What happened?

_____

_____

_____

_____

Did you resolve the argument?

_____

_____

_____

How did you feel? _____

How did your friend feel? _____

Rabbit

Rabbit likes to compromise so that both people in the conflict are happy. Rabbit hops back and forth. Both friends give up something. This is a helpful way to solve a disagreement.

Have you or a friend ever solved a disagreement like Rabbit? What happened?

_____

_____

_____

_____

Did you resolve the argument?

_____

_____

_____

How did you feel? _____

How did your friend feel? _____

Dog

Dog tries to make everyone happy so will give in when there is an argument. If you solve a disagreement like Dog, only one person will get what they want. The other person who gives in to make everyone else happy does not get what they want. This is an unhelpful way to solve a disagreement.

Have you or a friend ever tackled a disagreement like Dog? What happened?

_____

_____

_____

_____

Did you resolve the argument?

_____

_____

_____

How did you feel? _____

How did your friend feel? _____

Resolving Disagreements in 3 Steps

Step 1: Cool off.
Ask yourself, 'Am I ready to solve this problem?' If you are too angry or upset, give yourself a chance to calm and cool down. You may need to walk away or take a few deep breaths before coming back to solve the problem.

Step 2: Listen.
Listen to your friend tell their side of the story. Let your friend know that you understood what they were saying by telling them what you heard. Start with, 'I heard you say…' When you are telling your side of the story, try to use 'I' messages.

Step 3: Solve.
Talk about possible solutions until you find a compromise or a solution. If you are having trouble solving the problem, ask an adult for help.

When you are solving a disagreement, it is really important to use 'I' messages and not 'you' messages. Starting a disagreement with 'you' can make the other person angry and defensive. It can look like you are blaming and accusing your friend. It also shows no ownership of your feelings.

Emily took Noah's glue stick without asking permission. Noah told Emily, 'You always take my things'. Emily angrily replied, 'You never let me use your things'.

Noah and Emily used 'you' messages. Instead, Noah could have said, 'I want you to ask me before taking my things'. Emily may not have become angry and defensive if Noah used an 'I' message instead of a 'you' message.

Can you think of an 'I' message that Emily could have said back to Noah?

_____

_____

_____

Using 'I' and not 'You' messages takes a lot of practice!

135

Solving a disagreement like Owl

How could you solve the following disagreements?

It is lunch time. Your friend wants to play a game of soccer, but you want to play in the sand pit.

_____

_____

_____

You and your friend are playing handball. The ball bounces twice in your square. Your friend calls, 'You're out!' You argue with your friend that your rules are different and the ball is allowed to bounce twice.

_____

_____

_____

Your friend takes your pencil without asking.

_____

_____

_____

BEFORE YOU SPEAK THINK AND BE SMART, IT IS HARD TO FIX A WRINKLED HEART

137

Lesson Ten

Be Kind

In a world where you can be anything...

BE KIND

One Kind Word

Did you know that one kind word can change someone's entire day? It can change your day, too. When you are kind, your brain releases a hormone called oxytocin. Oxytocin makes you feel good. This means the kinder you are the better you feel and the happier you are.

Think about your day today and answer the following questions.

Think of someone who was kind to you today. What happened?

_____

_____

_____

How did this person make you feel?

_____

_____

_____

Think of someone you were kind to today. What happened?

_____

_____

_____

How do you think it made them feel?

_____

_____

_____

How did it make you feel?

_____

_____

_____

Two things happen when you are kind.

1. You warm someone's heart.

2. **You also warm your heart.**

Your kind act makes someone feel good and it comes right back to you!

Kindness Scale

The Kindness Scale measures how full your heart is. When your heart is bursting with love you want to share your happiness. Warming someone else's heart will warm your heart even more! However, sometimes a person is at the bottom of the kindness scale with a heart that has no love to give, and they may start to say or do unkind things to other people. A heart with no love to give can sometimes make people do unkind things. Unfortunately, being unkind will not warm someone's heart and will not warm your heart, either.

Bursting with love heart.

Warm heart.

Half-full Heart.

Cold heart.

No love to give heart.

Do you remember a time when you or someone you know was unkind? What happened?

_____

_____

_____

_____

_____

How did it make you feel?

_____

_____

How do you think it made the other person feel?

_____

_____

_____

Having a heart with no love to give does not make it okay to be unkind. Being mean and bullying is never okay.

Is It Bullying?

How do you know if you or someone else is being bullied? There is a difference between a disagreement (which we have just learned about), joking around and bullying.

Disagreement

When two people are having an argument or disagreement and a solution can usually be found.

Joking Around

When everyone is having fun and participating equally. Most importantly, no one is getting hurt.

One-Time Thing

When someone is being mean on purpose but it happens once and doesn't repeat itself.

Bullying

When someone is being mean on purpose and it happens again and again.

Can you remember a time when you and your friends were joking around? What happened?

_____

_____

_____

_____

Can you remember a time when you or someone you know was mean on purpose, but it only happened once?

_____

_____

_____

_____

Can you remember a time when you or someone you know was mean on purpose, and it happened more than once?

_____

_____

_____

_____

Ask your journal mate if they can remember a time they were bullied.

How to Face a Bully

1. Maintain eye contact.
2. Keep your voice calm and even.
3. Stand an appropriate distance.
4. Use the bully's name.

Say things like.....

Not cool.

Knock it off!

That is not a funny joke.

Friends don't do that.

Cut it out.

That was not funny.

It is important to use a strong, calm voice. It is also important to NOT say something mean back to the bully.

What would you do...?

You are drawing at your desk when a bully comes up to you and scribbles on your work.

_____

_____

_____

You are playing in the playground, when a bully kicks your ball over the fence.

_____

_____

_____

During playtime you ask your friends to play, but a bully tells you that you can't play and that no one likes you.

_____

_____

_____

You are walking to the toilets, when a bully pushes past you and makes you fall over.

_____

_____

It is very important to tell an adult if someone is bullying you. The adult may be a teacher that you trust and who you know will listen to you. The adult may be your mother, your father or your grandmother. Tattling is very different from reporting. Let's look a little closer at the difference between them.

Tattling   VERSUS   Reporting

Tattling	Reporting
• Getting someone in trouble.	• Keeping someone safe.
• Behaviour you are reporting on is an accident.	• Behaviour you are reporting is on purpose.
• It's harmless.	• It's dangerous.
• Can be solved on its own.	• Need help from an adult
• Not important.	• Important.

Can you think of an example of tattling and an example of reporting?

_____

_____

_____

_____

Warming a Heart

Write a mini thank you note to give to someone special to you.
It is a sure way to warm their heart and brighten their day!

Write a draft of your thank you note below.

_____

_____

_____

_____

_____

You've Got GRIT!

Congratulations! You have finished your Get GRIT journal. Reflect on what you have learned by answering the following questions.

What did you like learning about in your Get GRIT journal?

_____

_____

What did you learn that has helped you the most?

_____

_____

What skills do you need to practice?

_____

_____

What does GRIT mean to you?

_____

_____

_____

_____

_____

I HAVE GRIT.

I have a **positive attitude.**

I believe I can do anything I set my mind to.

I have a GROWTH MINDSET.

I believe challenges will make me smarter.

I dream BIG.

I am PERSISTENT and RESILIENT.

I am the boss of my thoughts. I catch negative 'I Can't' thoughts and change them to **positive 'I Can' thoughts.**

I share, take turns and I'm honest with my friends.

I play to WIN friendships.

I am BRAVE and I stand up for myself.

I HAVE GRIT.

ABOUT THE AUTHOR

Michele Lund

The *Get GRIT* program was developed by school guidance counsellor Michele Lund in response to parents and teachers seeking a program that teaches children the necessary social and emotional skills to successfully navigate school and life. With over a decade of school-based experience as a classroom teacher, a learning support teacher and in her current position as a guidance counsellor, Michele recognised the need to provide a social skills and resilience program which focused on developing healthy relationships and a positive growth mindset. Many of the children Michele works with experience low self-esteem, anxiety, poor social skills, and a fixed mindset. Michele, a mother of 2 young children herself, is passionate about teaching and inspiring children to be resilient, determined, to tackle life's challenges with grit, develop a growth mindset and reach their true potential.

Lightning Source UK Ltd.
Milton Keynes UK
UKHW020615060319

338567UK00004B/20/P